IMAGES
of America

ROUTE 66 IN THE
MISSOURI OZARKS

D0922425

These bathing beauties pose at Stoneydell Resort, one mile west of Arlington. Stoneydell included a huge pool beautifully constructed with Ozark rock, a restaurant, a service station, and 10 cabins. There was even a justice of the peace on duty. It was such a popular destination that the highway patrol directed traffic every weekend. (Author's collection.)

On the cover: The 4 Acre Court east of Lebanon is an example of a common construction style that gave the Ozarks a unique look. Cabins, gas stations, and cafés were often constructed of materials close at hand, particularly sandstone slabs. Grout that was sometimes painted white or black filled the gaps, giving the building a distinctive "giraffe rock" veneer. Please see page 53. (Author's collection.)

IMAGES
of America

ROUTE 66 IN THE MISSOURI OZARKS

Joe Sonderman

ARCADIA
PUBLISHING

Copyright © 2009 by Joe Sonderman
ISBN 978-0-7385-6030-4

Published by Arcadia Publishing
Charleston, South Carolina

Printed in the United States of America

Library of Congress Control Number: 2008943365

For all general information contact Arcadia Publishing at:
Telephone 843-853-2070
Fax 843-853-0044
E-mail sales@arcadiapublishing.com
For customer service and orders:
Toll-Free 1-888-313-2665

Visit us on the Internet at www.arcadiapublishing.com

CONTENTS

Acknowledgments   6

Introduction   7

1.   Crawford County   9

2.   Phelps County   17

3.   Pulaski County   35

4.   Laclede County   51

5.   Webster County   65

6.   Greene County   71

7.   Lawrence County   103

8.   Jasper County   109

ACKNOWLEDGMENTS

Special thanks to Tommy and Glenda Pike of the Route 66 Association of Missouri for their guidance. The work by Jim Powell for the Route 66 Association of Missouri magazine *Show Me Route 66* and from *The Missouri U.S. 66 Tour Book* by C. H. "Skip" Curtis is invaluable. Also thanks to Bill Wheeler, Karla Curtis, the staff of the Missouri State Archives, Cathy Dane at the Lebanon Library, Jane Lee at the Missouri Department of Transportation, and Michele Newton Hansford at the Powers Museum in Carthage. Jim Ross, Shellee Graham, Ron Warnick, and Jerry McClanahan also provided valuable input. Unless otherwise noted, all images are courtesy of the author.

INTRODUCTION

The Ozarks are one of the top tourist destinations in the United States, from the coves of the Lake of the Ozarks to the glitz of Branson. Route 66 served as the gateway to this vacation wonderland. It also brought our brave men and women of the military to train at Fort Leonard Wood and enabled truckers to bring all manner of bounty to the great cities. Route 66 is still there. It is for those of us who like to savor the scenery, to return to a time when getting there was half the fun.

In 1900, the Missouri Ozarks had changed very little since 1821, when Henry Rowe Schoolcraft wrote, "The traveler in the interior is often surprised to behold, at one view cliffs and prairies, bottoms and barrens, naked hills, heavy forests, streams and plains, all succeeding one another with rapidity and with pleasing harmony." The French called the plateau *aux Arks*, an abbreviation of the phrase meaning "to Arkansas."

Only rutted trails penetrated the wilderness, but resorts were springing up along the Gasconade and Big Piney Rivers serviced by the St. Louis and San Francisco (Frisco) Railroad. They were a popular destination for wealthy sportsmen from the big cities. The automobile finally opened up the Ozarks to the masses.

The road that became U.S. 66 was actually a network of Native American trails. In 1837, the state authorized a road between St. Louis and Springfield following the Kickapoo Trail or Osage Trail. In the 1840s, the federal government established a stagecoach line between St. Louis and Springfield. The route became known as the Wire Road after the telegraph lines went up. It was a vital military thoroughfare during the Civil War, carrying troops to battle at Wilson's Creek, at Carthage, and in hundreds of skirmishes.

Since most travel after the Civil War was by rail, it would be some time before the roads became an issue. It was actually the bicyclists who began pushing for better roads. The first automobiles came to Missouri in 1891, and there were over 16,000 registered by 1911.

In 1917, an association laid out the Ozark Trail from St. Louis to Romeroville, New Mexico. From there, it joined the National Old Trails Road to Los Angeles. At that time, promoters were laying out a myriad of routes with catchy names. Travelers often found themselves routed miles out of their way because towns or businesses paid to be on the route.

By 1920, a segment of roadway had been paved from Webb City through Joplin. It would become part of the state highway system, organized in 1922. The route between St. Louis and the Kansas line was designated as Missouri Route 14.

Cyrus Avery of Oklahoma, the man who originally envisioned Route 66, sought help from John T. Woodruff. Woodruff was a Springfield civic leader and owner of the Kentwood Arms Hotel, whom Avery had known in the Ozark Trails Association. They landed spots on a committee that assigned the route numbers for the proposed federal highway system in 1925.

The Committee of the American Association of State Highway and Transportation Officials assigned even numbers to the east–west highways, with the most important routes ending in 0. The highway between Chicago and Los Angeles was assigned the number 60, and Missouri printed thousands of maps showing that designation. But Kentucky officials demanded that 60 be assigned to a highway from Newport News, Virginia, through their state. A standoff ensued until John Page, Oklahoma's chief engineer, noticed that the catchy-sounding 66 was still unused. At a meeting in Springfield on April 30, 1926, Missouri and Oklahoma officials proposed that 66 be assigned to the highway from Chicago to Los Angeles. Springfield can thus lay claim to being the birthplace of Route 66. The federal numbering system went into effect on November 11, 1926.

Avery and Woodruff invited representatives from the Route 66 states to form an association in Tulsa on February 4, 1927. Woodruff became the first president of the U.S. Highway 66 Association, which coined the phrase "The Main Street of America." With Missouri Route 14 becoming U.S. 66 and Missouri Route 5 becoming U.S. 65, Woodruff said Springfield was the new "crossroads of America."

The association's publicity man came up with the idea of a transcontinental footrace to build awareness of Route 66. Promoted by C. C. Pyle, the Bunion Derby made Route 66 front-page news. Nearly 300 runners started in Los Angeles on March 4, 1928, entering Missouri on Route 66 on April 21. Pyle charged fees for towns to host this traveling circus. When negotiations to have the race stop in Carthage failed, he opted for Miller instead. Angry residents of Carthage pelted the lead cars with eggs. The runners arrived in Rolla on April 25 and made it to St. Louis on April 29. The city refused to pay for the race to stop there, so the runners stayed in East St. Louis. Only 55 runners were left when Andy Payne from the Route 66 town of Foyil, Oklahoma, crossed the line first in New York on May 26. Payne won $25,000, and "Cash and Carry" Pyle went broke.

Missouri was the third state to completely pave Route 66 within its borders. The final section was completed on January 5, 1931, near Arlington. More than 8,000 people attended a celebration in Rolla on March 15 to mark the occasion. Even during the height of the Great Depression, the Ozarks saw increases in tourist traffic, due to the completion of the Bagnell Dam on May 30, 1931. It created what was then the largest man-made lake in the nation, a short drive from Route 66.

The construction of Fort Leonard Wood caused a massive increase in traffic. In 1939, 119 cars used the intersection of Route 66 and Missouri Route 17 during a 24-hour period. That number had soared to 16,375 by March 1941. During the first nine months of 1941, 54 people died in crashes on Route 66 in Phelps, Pulaski, and Laclede Counties. That toll includes a fiery crash involving a troop-carrying army truck near Hazelgreen on August 10, 1941, that killed nine soldiers and a civilian truck driver. The first major section of four-lane divided highway on Route 66 bypassed the most treacherous stretch through Devil's Elbow in 1943.

After the war, the soldiers returned home to bring their families to the Ozark vacationland or California. These were the glory years of Route 66. But change was coming. On August 2, 1956, Missouri became the first state to award a contract with the new funds from the Interstate Highway Act. The first contract signed was for work on Route 66, now Interstate 44, in Laclede County.

Missouri was not giving up on Route 66 just yet. In December 1962, the state petitioned federal officials to designate the route between Chicago and Los Angeles as Interstate 66. The feds refused. Interstate 44 was completed across Missouri by 1967. On January 17, 1977, Route 66 was decertified between Chicago and Joplin. Joplin served as the eastern terminus until the highway was completely decertified in 1985.

But the old road would not die. On July 10, 1990, Gov. John Ashcroft came to Waynesville and Springfield to sign legislation designating Route 66 as a historic roadway. Missouri was the first state to enact such a measure, aimed at preserving Route 66 for future generations.

One

CRAWFORD COUNTY

Bourbon is famous for its three water towers labeled "Bourbon." The name dates from the 1850s, when Richard Turner sold whiskey to railroad construction crews at his store. The business became known as the Bourbon Store. Alex and Edith Mortenson opened the Bourbon Lodge in 1932. It is now a private home, and the cabins are in ruins.

Alex and Edith Mortenson later opened the High Hill Tourist Court just west of the Bourbon Lodge. It included a store, a Texaco station, and four cabins. The three single cabins went for $3 per night, and the double cost $5. Jewell and Lillian Heitman took over from the Mortensons in 1947 and ran the operation until 1955. The house and one cabin still stand.

Oscar Roedemeier took over the Souder Brothers Garage in 1925. The complex would later be expanded to include Sweeney's Steak House, operated by R. D. Sweeney and his wife. They advertised "The home of good steaks and chicken. Our steers—and our guests—are well fed." Oscar's son Kermit and his wife Faye ran a motel across the street.

10

Onondaga (Iroquois for "spirit of the mountain") opened to St. Louis and San Francisco (Frisco) Railroad tourists in 1904. A bitter rivalry developed in 1932 as William and Lee Mook marketed the cave beneath their land as Missouri Caverns, while Bob Bradford ran Onondaga. Missouri Caverns closed during World War II. Lester Dill and Lyman Riley, owners of Meramec Caverns, took over in 1953. Onondaga became a state park in 1982.

Cuba is known as "Mural City, USA" with numerous colorful murals illustrating the history of the town. The Red Horse opened in 1938 and was operated by Mr. and Mrs. C. C. Cox. The station/garage building later became a truck stop but was destroyed by fire in 1953. A few of the cabins still stand. The adjacent home has been moved a bit west.

11

The Wagon Wheel Motel opened in 1934 as the Wagon Wheel Cabins. St. Louis stonemason Leo Friesenhan designed the buildings for Robert and Margaret Martin. The original 10 units grew to 14 by the time the Martins sold the Wagon Wheel in 1946. John and Winifred Pratt ran the motel from 1947 to 1963.

Pauline Roberts and her husband Hallie took over the Wagon Wheel in 1963. Hallie died in 1980, and Pauline married Harold Armstrong in 1988. Along with caretaker Roy Mudd, they made the Wagon Wheel a Route 66 icon. The Wagon Wheel is one of the best-preserved authentic Route 66 motels.

Chester's Café and the Cooke Service Station opened in 1944 as the Wagon Wheel Annex. The café was later known as Paul's, for owner Paul Killeen. Killeen later changed the name to the Annex Café. The business closed in 1965, after Interstate 44 was completed. Missouri Hick BBQ now stands on the site.

Cuba was founded in 1857, in anticipation of the construction of the Frisco Railroad. The town received its name after two former California gold miners impressed residents with tales about their holiday on the "Isle of Cuba." This view looks east past the People's Bank, the City Hotel, and Barnett Motor Company.

Constructed in 1915, the Palace Hotel faced the Frisco Railroad tracks and the Old Springfield Road, later Missouri Route 14. When Route 66 was constructed, an entrance was added in the back to face the new road. The name was later changed to the Hotel Cuba. The hotel had 20 "Steam Heated and Air Cooled Rooms."

The Cuba Drug Store on the "East End Square" sold liquors and offered fountain service. The building later housed Diane's Corner Lounge, then the Route 66 Lounge, and is now the East Office Lounge. The Cuba Theatre is on the left. Dr. J. A. Bland's dentist office and Suzies Café are on the right. Note the panel van delivering gin.

John Mullen owned the Midway Garage and Star Café, constructed in the 1920s. Allyne Earls took over operation in 1934. In the 1940s, a second floor was added and the garage was eliminated. Earls never closed the doors until 1972. Noel Picard, St. Louis Blues hockey player and broadcaster, owned the Midway from 1976 to 1983.

Arthur and Mary Ruth Eads ran the Midway for a time before opening the Eads Café in 1930. It was filled with stuffed animal heads, Native American artifacts, and old guns. New owner Bill Wiese named it the B and M in 1942, for Bill and his stepdaughter Mary. The building later housed the Church of Jesus Christ Foundation, with its highway shield sign proclaiming, "Jesus—King of the Road."

Serafino and Mary Vitali opened the Fanning Store on the left in 1930. Mary's brother Joe Bacialli built the store and the adjacent Speedway Garage, later Joe's Place Tavern, and the Fanning Social Club. The store closed in 1972 and was torn down in the 1980s. The site is now the Fanning Outpost General Store, home of the 44-foot-tall rocking chair, the world's largest.

Henry and Elsie Belle King constructed this roadside stand at the top of King's Hill on what is now Route ZZ, west of Cuba, in the 1940s. It was located next to their rock house, which still stands. King's sold pottery, Ozark baskets, souvenirs, and even fresh eggs. A second home now occupies the former location of the stand.

Two

PHELPS COUNTY

Route 66 is marked as Route KK into St. James, where a friendly face greeted motorists at Jim Foote's Standard station. The area was originally known as Big Prairie. It was to have been named Jamestown, in honor of Thomas James, who owned the nearby Meramec Iron Works. But the name was already taken, so *Saint* was added. His granddaughter, Lucy Wortham James, donated the land that became Meramec Springs Park. (James Memorial Library.)

Thomas Biles opened the Atlasta service station just east of St. James in August 1929. It had a coffee shop, lunch counter, and gas station downstairs. A dance and banquet hall was upstairs, and there were cabins in the back. The building at left was a tire shop. All but the tire shop burned to the ground on July 18, 1964. (James Memorial Library.)

John and Mable Rose operated the Rose Café in St. James beginning in 1929. It was later known as the Commercial Café and is Mary's Cafe in this 1951 view. In 1960, John Bullock took over and turned it into Johnnie's Bar and Indian Relic Museum. The bar with its old Stag Beer sign is still open today and is run by Johnnie's son, Russ.

This view looks east from the first divided section of Route 66 in Missouri at St. James. The landowner, identified only as Mr. Pace, would not sell unless the state built a divided boulevard. Charles Bremmer's market is on the left with George Hamilton's Shell station at right. This section is now cut off by Interstate 44, just to the west. (James Memorial Library.)

Mr. and Mrs. "Pop" Scherer's Night and Day Café was open around the clock. "We serve everything in season with no substitutes." They offered telephone, mail, and Western Union service. The original building was much smaller and was known for pit barbecue. This 1950s postcard view notes that they served "fine food with T.V."

Frank Ebling founded the Mule Trading Post in Pacific in 1946. Ebling moved his business to Rolla in 1957 after Interstate 44 bypassed Pacific. The billboards featuring the friendly mule were found as far away as Joplin. Carl and Zelma Smith run the classic trading post, and the mule still wiggles his neon ears today off Interstate 44 at exit 189.

Ramey's Café was built in the late 1930s just west of the junction of Route 66 and U.S. 63. (Bishop Avenue). Ramey's became a popular hangout for local college students and was later turned into a tavern. It burned down in 1970, and the Laborers Local 840 Union Hall now occupies the site.

Henry Clay Pierce of the Pierce Petroleum Company envisioned a chain of first-class facilities for travelers every 125 miles in the Ozarks when most roadside accommodations were rudimentary. The Pennant Hotel in Rolla opened on November 4, 1929. George Carney turned it into the Carney Motel in 1956. It became the Carney Manor in 1963, and the Drury Inn stands on the site today.

The Pierce-Pennant Tavern opened on August 1, 1928, and was originally operated by Diehl Montgomery and G. Fagen. After selling the Wagon Wheel Motel in Cuba in 1946, Robert and Margaret Martin turned the tavern into the Pennant Café and Hotel Martin. Badly damaged in a 1953 fire, it was demolished for a new Motel Martin, which no longer stands.

"Rolla's newest and finest" in 1938, Hull's Colonial Village included a 24-room hotel, a restaurant, and cabins in the back. It was later known as Frederick's and operated by Fred and Vernelle Gasser, who had also owned Vernelle's Motel near Arlington. Lee's Fried Chicken was later built here at 1902 North Bishop Avenue.

The Trav-L-odge Tourist Court and Steakhouse featured "Delicious broiled steaks and sea foods." The motel units were steam heated and approved by the Western Travelodge Hotel and Motel System. The Trav-L-odge was not connected with the familiar Travelodge chain. It was built well before the corporation was formed in 1946.

Richard E. Schuman opened his Tourist City in June 1929, reportedly converting some old chicken coops into cottages. The complex grew to include 40 units, a service station, and café. After a 1931 robbery, the grounds were patrolled at night by "a watchman who carries a watch clock which he punches at all stations on all parts of the court."

This view of Rolla about 1946 looks east from Route 66 and Pine Street (City 66) toward Schuman's Tourist City on the left and the Bell Café and Cafeteria and Greyhound depot on the right. The Pennant Café is visible behind the Bell. The Budget Deluxe Inn occupies the Schuman's Tourist City site today.

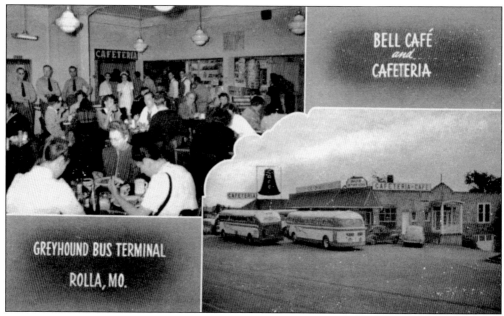

Robert Bell opened a garage in 1927 that grew into the Bell Café and Cafeteria. It was owned by Reginald Waters and managed by Andy Waterman when this view was made. It served as the original Greyhound and Missouri, Kansas and Oklahoma (MK&O) Bus Lines depot. The cafeteria closed in the 1950s and later became a flea market.

In 1947, a new bus depot and cafeteria were built next door to the Bell to compete with the nearby Pickwick bus terminal at the Pennant Cafe. Andy Waterman's café was "known coast to coast for our famous ham" and could seat 200 people. Waterman said they could feed four busloads of tourists in 45 minutes.

"New and Modern"
On U. S. Highway 66 and 63. Phelps Oil Company, Rolla, Missouri

The Phelps Oil Corporation constructed the Phelps Modern Cottages at Bishop Avenue and Thirteenth Street about 1934. It invited guests to "Sleep where sleeping is safe" in the 16 modern cottages at "one of the finest auto courts in the Ozarks." It was later known as the Grande Court, and a Dairy Queen was later built on the site.

Maurice Ernest Gillioz opened the Hotel Edwin Long on March 12, 1931. He named it for Sen. Edwin Long, who died in 1928. Just three days after opening, the hotel hosted the celebration marking the paving of Route 66 across Missouri. It housed the National Bank of Rolla, which became Phelps County Bank in 1960. The hotel had 75 rooms.

Rolla was laid out in 1855 as a supply point for the Frisco Railroad. George Coppedge suggested naming the community Raleigh after his hometown in North Carolina. Everyone agreed and spelled the name the way Coppedge pronounced it, "Rolla." This view of Pine Street (City 66) dates from 1945. (Missouri State Archives.)

This photograph of the west entrance to Rolla dates from prior to World War II and looks east. Route 66 and U.S. 63 (now Bishop Avenue) curve to the left. City Route 66 (Kingshighway Street) is shown running past the large letters spelling out "Rolla" on the right. City Route 66 used Pine Street and Sixth Street to Kingshighway Street.

The 1950s view of the same spot shows the results of the postwar boom. "Bud" Klinefelter's Ford, later Diehl Montgomery Ford and Denny Ford, is at left. Blockbuster Video now occupies the site of the farm implement dealership.

Zeno and Loretta Scheffer opened Zeno's Steak House and Motel in 1957. It originally featured 32 ultramodern units, along with wired music, a swimming pool, and a lounge. The motel at today's Interstate 44 and Martin Springs Road now features 50 newly remodeled rooms, banquet facilities, and the "award winning restaurant."

Harry and Edna Cochran opened a souvenir stand topped with a totem pole near Arlington in 1933. Ralph and Catherine Jones bought it in 1957. The business has relocated twice due to highway realignment. The present Totem Pole location on the west end of Rolla opened in 1977. The old totem pole stands inside. (Tim Jones.)

The Skillet Café and Cities Service station stood on Highway 66 West next to Dickmann's Wayfarer Inn. Vernon Key Palmer owned and managed the café and also operated the Spare Rib Inn in Steeleville for nearly 50 years before retiring in 1977. The Skillet advertised "Good Food at Sensible Prices."

Paul and Gladys Bramwell Bennett opened their restaurant just west of the intersection of Route 66 and the Newburg Road (Route T) in 1943. Gladys is serving customers in this view. An evangelist known as "the fishing, coon-hunting preacher of the Ozarks," Paul built a tabernacle out back. They moved the business to Clementine when four-lane Route 66 was constructed in 1952 and closed when Interstate 44 cut off access in 1967.

E. P. Gasser built the Gasser Tourist Court in 1938. Fred and Vernelle Gasser bought it from their uncle in 1952. The restaurant was relocated when the four-lane route was built in 1957 and demolished for Interstate 44 construction in 1968. Nye Goodridge took over in 1960, and his son Ed still operates the motel. The 2005 realignment of Interstate 44 was especially cruel to Vernelle's Motel, leaving it invisible from the interstate.

Bill and Bessie's Place, eight miles west of Rolla, included a dance hall and six log cabins, opened by Bill and Beatrice "Bessie" Bayless in 1931. On October 31, 1935, Eugene Duncan shot and killed his estranged wife Billie at the dance hall. John Dausch, known as "Sunday John" for illegally selling alcohol on Sundays, changed the name to John's Modern Cabins in 1951. The cabins have been deteriorating since he died in 1971.

An airline beacon topped the Beacon Hill Motel. The gas station and the original restaurant were torn down when the new four-lane route was built. The nine cabins were connected, and the restaurant shown here was then added. The Beacon closed after Interstate 44 left it marooned in 1968. The ruins were still visible from Interstate 44 in 2009.

Through the redrawing of county lines over the years, Arlington has been in St. Louis, Gasconade, Crawford, Pulaski, and Phelps Counties. Founded by P. C. Harrison, the village dates back to the 1860s and was once a popular resort destination on the Frisco Railroad. Interstate 44 construction in the 1960s left the picturesque hamlet accessible only by a winding dead-end service road, today's Arlington Outer Road.

Route 66 originally wound its way down the grade past the Arlington Tourists Camp. It then crossed a railroad bridge and a multiple truss bridge over the Little Piney River, built in 1923. This section east of the Pulaski County line near Arlington was the last segment of Route 66 in Missouri to be paved. It was finished on January 5, 1931. Workers tossed coins into the concrete to celebrate.

Looking east at Arlington Hill, the 1923 bridge is at right and the 1952 span creating four-lane Route 66 is at left. The 1923 bridge came down when Interstate 44 was constructed in 1966, and the 1952 bridge was replaced in 2005. (Missouri State Archives.)

Cherokee Indians forced to move from the southeastern United States to Oklahoma camped here on their bitter journey along the Trail of Tears in the 1830s. George Prewett constructed the amazing Stoneydell Resort and its 100-foot-long swimming pool in 1932. Stoneydell included a hotel, 10 cabins, a restaurant, a goldfish pond, and even a justice of the peace. Mae West once stopped here.

Fred Widener ran Stoneydell from 1954 to 1967, when everything on the south side was torn down for Interstate 44. The restaurant, later known as Pop's Stoneydell Café and Granny's Old Fashun Cookin', still stands on the north side. The goldfish pond, a couple of cabins, and the stone arch entrance also remain.

Pecan Joe's was part of a chain based in Texas. This location opened in 1960 and was "Headquarters for gifts of the Ozarks and Pecan Joe's famous candies." Victor and Jacki Lomax operated the business from 1964 until 1967, when Interstate 44 was constructed and the business was demolished. Note the trademark pecan wearing a cowboy hat.

The Powell Brothers, Jewell, Harry, and Herman, owned a trucking firm serving southwest Missouri and St. Louis. In the early 1930s, they constructed a 24-hour service station, restaurant, and store with 10 cabins that was actually marked on state road maps as Powellville. It was all torn down when Interstate 44 was constructed in 1967.

Phelps County businesses such as Pep's Place sold high-quality baskets woven from white oak strips by craftsmen like William and Henry Childers, Carl Becker, and Clarence Wells in the community of Clementine. The town became known as "Basketville." Basketville died out after construction of the four-lane highway.

Three

PULASKI COUNTY

Sterling Wells ran Wells Station on the old route in Hooker. He opened the Hillbilly Store on the new four-lane route in 1943. The business moved again when Interstate 44 was constructed in 1981. The original hillbilly sign with its rotating arms ended up in Willow Springs. The hillbilly built for the newer location is now at the Mule Trading Post.

The twisting highway through Hooker and Devil's Elbow could not handle the huge increase in traffic due to the construction of Fort Leonard Wood. Traffic between Waynesville and Rolla tripled between 1939 and 1941. A new four-lane highway bypassing Hooker and Devil's Elbow opened in 1943. This view shows crews from Fred Weber Construction of St. Louis working on the famous Hooker Cut. (Missouri Department of Transportation.)

This 1941 view of the cut construction is east toward Hooker. The old route is visible on the left. The village was named for sportsman John Hooker, whose camp was a popular sportsmen's destination. In 1929, the *St. Louis Post Dispatch* reported that Hooker had the smallest high school in Missouri. (Missouri State Archives.)

When it opened, the 90-foot-deep Hooker Cut was the largest rock cut in the United States. The angled curbs were designed to send rainwater to drains but actually often caused vehicles to overturn. This section is now County Route Z. The 1926 route through Hooker is now Trophy Lane and the original route into Devil's Elbow is now Teardrop Road.

In 1936, Nellie Munger married Emmett Moss, and they built a sandwich shop just east of the Devil's Elbow Bridge. Jessie and Pete Hudson later owned it but moved to Lebanon after Devil's Elbow was bypassed in 1943. Starting in 1946, Paul and Nadine Thompson ran it as the Elbow Inn. The inn closed in the 1960s. It reopened in 1997 and now offers some unique ceiling decorations—a collection of patrons' bras.

The state planning commission in 1941 named Devil's Elbow one of the Seven Beauty Spots of Missouri. The name was bestowed by lumberjacks floating logs past a sharp bend in the Big Piney River. They cursed it as "a devil of an elbow." Bypassed in 1943, Devil's Elbow is little changed today. The steel truss bridge was built in 1923. (Missouri Department of Transportation.)

Dwight Rench constructed this beautiful Ozark rock café and Conoco station just west of the bridge in 1932. It operated in conjunction with Rench's Cedar Lodge, offering 10 cottages. The Devil's Elbow Post Office was located here from 1933 to 1941. The building later became the Hideaway Tavern but burned to the ground in 1974.

Atholl "Jiggs" Miller built Miller's Market in 1954, next to the camp operated by his father-in-law, Charles McCoy. He moved the post office from McCoy's Camp. Terry and Marilyn Allman ran the store as Allman's Market from 1982 to 2001 before it was purchased by Phil Sheldon. The tiny post office is still in operation.

Charles McCoy built his store and camp in 1941. He rented boats and sold fishing equipment, and this building was the post office beginning in 1941. The building became apartments, and the post office moved to Miller's Market in 1954. McCoy's had six rooms upstairs, and seven cabins were added in 1948.

DANCING, FISHING, HUNTING, SHADY
TRAILER CAMP, DINNERS, LUNCHES, BEER
MODERN CABINS WITH IN-SPR. MATTRESS

E161   ERNIE & ZADA'S INN   HI-WAY 66   1 MILE WEST OF   DEVIL'S ELBOW, MO.   Schuster Studio Hermann, Mo.

Originally known as Clinton Cabins, Ernie and Zada's Inn opened in 1932 and became a well-known honky-tonk. But it was only in business for a couple of years. It was later known as Grandview Court, now Grandview Trailer Park. The canopy of the gas station has been enclosed, and three of the cabins still stand.

This view shows the 1943 four-lane Route 66 (now Route Z) crossing the new bridge over the Big Piney River. The divided four-lane highway through the Hooker cut and across this bridge was the first major four-lane section to be built and the last section of Route 66 to be bypassed. The new Interstate 44 here opened in January 1981.

Old Route 66 originally went straight where it now meets the 1943 four-lane highway west of Devil's Elbow, passing through Morgan Heights. The Morgan Heights Tourist Hotel also offered cabins for $1 to $1.50 per night during the 1930s. Travelers today can wander a short stretch of the original two-lane highway between the north side of Interstate 44 and Missouri Route 28.

This view shows the intersection of Route 66 and Missouri Route 28 at Morgan Heights before the roadways were paved. Looking northeast, Route 28 swung off to the left toward Dixon, while Route 66 continued down the hill toward Devil's Elbow. The station was a stop for the Pickwick Stages Bus Line, which merged with Greyhound in 1929.

After Fort Leonard Wood was built, a string of businesses eager to serve the soldiers sprang up at the turn off from Route 66. The area in this May 1941 image was originally known as Gospel Ridge. St. Robert was incorporated in 1951, after the Reverend Robert J. Arnold established a church named for St. Robert Bellarmine. (Missouri State Archives.)

Fort Leonard Wood was named after a Medal of Honor winner who went on to become U.S. Army chief of staff. This view is to the north from M Avenue and Engineer Circle. Over three million people have trained here since 1940. Fort Wood is now the Army Maneuvers Support Center and training post for the engineer, chemical, and military police corps.

James Egan opened the Wagon Wheel Station and Café in the 1920s. It sold Barnsdall Gasoline and was open 24 hours a day. Egan's promised "Good Coffee— Always" and offered chicken dinners for 75¢ in the 1950s. It later became a nightclub. The Ramada Inn Fort Wood occupies this site today.

The Scott Garage was constructed about 1928. Dorsey Scott put up this elaborate rock front after the construction of Fort Leonard Wood. In addition to food and drinks, Scott's also offered "dime-a-dance" girls. It was all torn down for construction of Interstate 44. The site is now the parking lot of the Ramada Inn. (Missouri State Archives.)

Jodie and Herman Paulette opened their café in the early 1940s two miles east of Waynesville. They specialized in home-cooked foods and "Hot Biscuits Served 24 Hours." "Your Favorite Drinks" were available in the Elbow Room on the right side of the café. The café stood to the right of the present-day Pontiac dealership.

Neil "Doc" Williams somehow heard about the plans for Fort Leonard Wood ahead of time. Perhaps it was just a coincidence that he was friends with Sen. Harry Truman. In 1940, he opened the seven-cabin Oakwood Village two miles east of Waynesville. It was torn down for construction of Interstate 44, and a gas station is on the site today.

Mr. and Mrs. Leo Ablin said their Park 'N' Eat was home of the "world's largest hamburger," specializing in steaks, barbecue, chicken, and seafood with complete fountain service. The restaurant had a large dining room and offered curb service with food "prepared in sight must be right." It burned down in the 1970s.

Waynesville was laid out in 1839 and named for Gen. "Mad Anthony" Wayne. The 1941 WPA guide said it had "a leisurely atmosphere, unmarred by the smoke of industry and the impatient panting of trains, and but little jarred by farmer's Saturday night visits." As this view shows, that changed when Fort Leonard Wood was built.

The original Pulaski County Courthouse flew the Confederate flag from the spring of 1861 until federal troops arrived in June 1862. This courthouse was built in 1903 and served until 1993. It is now a museum. In 1990, Missouri governor John Ashcroft came here to sign a bill designating Route 66 as a historic highway.

When four-lane Route 66/Interstate 44 was constructed, the route through Waynesville was designated as City 66. The 1,234-seat Fort Wood Theatre opened on April 17, 1941. The owner said the theater "Compares with the largest in Springfield and Jefferson City." The theater closed in 1980. It was damaged by a flood and torn down.

Travel on Route 66 could be treacherous during the winter months. Waynesville and the Missouri Ozarks were draped in a blanket of white on November 6–7, 1951. A record 14.1 inches fell in Springfield. St. Louis recorded 12.5 inches, the greatest 24-hour snowfall there since 1912. Thousands of travelers were stranded.

Robert A. Bell, a local lawyer and judge, expanded his home into a hotel in 1925 to serve the expected tourist trade from Route 66. The Bell advertised "Every Facility for the Traveler's Pleasure" and "Old Southern Hospitality." The family operated it until 1937. It is now the Memorial Chapel of Waynesville funeral home.

The Bell family ran a café and camp next to the hotel, offering a garage and nine cabins. Mr. and Mrs. W. L. Thomas later operated it, keeping the Bell name and inviting travelers to "Sleep in Safety and Comfort." The service station building later became a floral shop and still stands today in front of the funeral home.

Hamilton's Pleasant Grove cabins were brand new when this photograph was taken in 1932. At that time, there was a Sinclair station and five cottages with cooking facilities renting for $1 to $1.50 per night. Rudy and Clara Schuermann later owned the property. The Bell family bought it in 1948 and changed the name to Bell Haven Court.

Route 66 passes through Buckhorn, named after a tavern that served the stagecoach line. A pair of deer antlers hung over the door. The road then passed the Buffalo Lick Camp at Laquey. "Lake-way" is named after Joseph Laquey, who used his political pull to obtain a post office. Early Route 66 followed today's Routes P and AA through town.

Caldwell's started out as a building divided into two parts, a café and a store/gas station. There were four little cabins in the back, three of which remain. This interior view shows the selection of novelties for sale. The expanded structure later became the Caldwell-Salsman Truck Stop and later the Gascozark Trading Post.

Frank A. Jones built the Gascozark Café. Rudy and Clara Schuermann operated it in the 1930s. It was covered in distinctive Ozark rock in 1939 and became the Greyhound bus stop. It was known for a fine selection of homemade baskets. The Gascozark became the Spinning Wheel Tavern in the 1950s. The abandoned building is still there.

Four

LACLEDE COUNTY

The Gasconade is the longest river flowing entirely within Missouri and one of the most crooked in the United States. It meanders through Webster, Texas, Wright, Laclede, Pulaski, Dent, Maries, Osage, Phelps, and Gasconade Counties for 271 miles to the Missouri River. The original bridge, still in use, was built in 1922. Construction of the new bridge for four-lane Route 66/Interstate 44 is underway in this June 1956 photograph. (Missouri State Archives.)

The Harbor Truck Port and Modern Cabins was built about 1939, just west of the junction with Route T. It later became Brownie's Truck Stop, then Andy's Midway. When Andy's opened at a new location across the highway, Geno Matella turned it into Geno's Tavern. The roadhouse building burned down in 1965.

Loren and Norma Alloway ran the general store in Sleeper for nearly 50 years before opening the Satellite Café in 1965. Prior to the Interstate 44 construction, the café was accessible from both sides of the four-lane highway. Leroy Hawkins sold Phillips 66 products at the "Space Station." It burned down in 1999.

Ray Coleman and Blackie Waters opened the 4 Acre Court in 1939. The giraffe rock buildings were billed as "family units and campground." They advertised, "After a Long Day's Drive—A Clean Motor Inn." One of the cabins was destroyed by a blaze in 2003, but the others are still rented out by the month.

The Vesta Court was opened in 1937 and operated by Clayton Lein beginning in 1942. Marie and Bill Williams bought the property in 1957 and named it the El Rancho Court, later a mobile home park. Only the foundations of the café remain today.

Dennis Scott opened Scotty's Tourist City in the mid-1940s and reportedly managed the business from his car. Scotty's stood just east of where the Elks Lodge is now and consisted of three cabins, a café, and a Skelly station/liquor store. The café offered just nine items, from a 25¢ hamburger to a southern fried chicken dinner for $1.

Elsie and Lee Kimes were bilked into buying a tourist camp west of Springfield that was about to be bypassed. They sold at a loss and bought the Green Gables in 1941. The cabins had attached garages, and each had its own plumbing. The Green Gables was expanded into the Forest Manor Motel, which is still in business today.

Jessie and Pete Hudson sold the Munger-Moss Sandwich Shop in Devil's Elbow and bought the Chicken Shanty Café in Lebanon in 1945. They renamed it the Munger Moss Barbecue and opened the motel in 1946. Bob and Ramona Lehman have operated this treasure since 1971, and Ramona has decorated some of the rooms in Route 66 themes.

Charles Clark's Rock Court offered 10 "Strictly Modern Rock Cabins among the trees." When Mr. and Mrs. Fred Parthier were running the place, there were 16 cabins and the café was "rocked" to match. It burned in 1965, and one cabin stands today behind the Wyota Inn.

G. E. and Laura Wrinkle started the Cedar Bluff resort at Hazelgreen in 1913 and then ran the Jefferson Hotel and Café in Lebanon starting in 1929. G. E. began building a new two-story hotel in 1946 but fell ill after completing one story. His son Glenn established Wrink's Market there in 1950, and his personality made the store a landmark. Glenn died in 2007, but his son Terry now runs the store. (Terry Wrinkle.)

William and Ethel Lenz turned their 14-room mansion into a tourist home in 1932. They offered amenities not found at the early tourist camps. As automobile camps improved and motorists began avoiding hotels, they changed the name to the Lenz Homotel. William and Ethel kept it open until 1975. (Missouri State Archives.)

Emis Spears, his wife Lois, and his parents opened Camp Joy in 1927. The family spent three days counting out-of-state cars passing by before buying the eight-acre site. Their daughter Joy was named after the camp, which once hosted Bonnie Parker, Clyde Barrow, and Pretty Boy Floyd. One of the drive-through signs urged, "Teach Your Baby to Say Camp Joy." The Spears family ran it until 1971.

In 1946, Andy Liebl converted two old streetcars from Springfield, Missouri, into Andy's Street Car Grill. It was located on the north side of Elm Street at Jackson Avenue and boasted of serving "the finest foods in the Ozarks" and "famous fried domestic rabbit." Andy's was demolished in 1961, following the relocation of Route 66.

The first of three service stations operated by O. E. Carter and Ed Lawson opened in 1935 at Route 66 and Washington Street. This building operated as a gas station until 1971, when Dean Elmore moved his Orchard Hills Package Store here from its original 1946 location on Route 66. The business remains in the family today. (Lebanon-Laclede County Library.)

Looking east on Route 66 at Missouri Route 5, Joe Knight's streamlined bus terminal, Standard station, and restaurant are on the left. A dramatic increase in traffic on Route 66 made it necessary for Knight to move the station here from his drugstore at Commercial and Madison Streets in 1941. Later known as the Metro Building, the terminal was torn down to make room for a Walgreen's.

Honorary colonel Arthur T. Nelson donated right-of-way through his apple orchard for the new Missouri Route 14, later Route 66. He opened this beautifully landscaped Texaco station on July 3, 1926. Nelson rented tents to travelers at first and then built the Top O' the Ozarks Inn. It originally had eight cabins named for each of the Route 66 states. The Missouri cabin still stands behind an antique store at 1211 West Elm Street. (Lebanon-Laclede County Library.)

Colonel Nelson opened a new building on January 21, 1930. He called it the Nelson Tavern, even though no alcohol was served. Travelers went miles out of their way to see the fantastic gardens that included 165 varieties of gladiolus. The fragrant interior was also filled with exotic plants and birds. "Nelsonville" was demolished in 1958, and the site is now a supermarket. (Lebanon-Laclede County Library.)

In 1933, Col. Arthur T. Nelson saw a musical fountain at the Chicago world's fair. He said that a design for a V-shaped tourist court with the fountain in the middle came to him in a dream in 1934. Across Route 66 from Nelsonville, records played over a loudspeaker as colored lights lit the fountain. His Dream Village was in business until 1977. The girl beside the fountain in this view is Beth Nelson Owen. (Lebanon-Laclede County Library.)

In 1949, Dave Caldwell of Richland bought the old Claxton Hotel and established Caldwell's Truck Stop and Café. His son-in-law Barney Brown took over in 1954. Caldwell's operated until 1971, and this site is now a car dealership. Note the tanker trucks parked close to the highway in this 1957 view looking east toward the Nelson Tavern. (Missouri State Archives.)

THE SILENT NITE TOURIST HOME
Simmons Beauty Rest Mattresses
Mr. and Mrs. J. D. Stanton, Props.
Hiway 66   Lebanon, Missouri

12150

Architect Jerry Louis designed the unusual Silent Night Tourist Home for James D. and Myrtle Stanton after they acquired the site in September 1937. In 1958, the building became L. N. Carter's Chiropractic Clinic. Dr. C. Norman Unverzagt opened his chiropractic center in the building at 331 West Elm Street in 1971.

LEBANON

On August 2, 1956, the first contract in the nation under the Interstate Highway Act was awarded for the new Route 66/Interstate 44 through Laclede County. A 4.6-mile section of four-lane highway bypassing Lebanon opened on August 8, 1957. The chamber of commerce erected the 14-by-40-foot signs promoting the town with "15,000 Friendly Folks."

61

Jessie Floyd Caffey constructed the first gas station on Missouri Route 14 between St. Louis and Springfield in 1924. Caffeyville grew to include a café, motel, campground, and feed mill. The W. A. Kay family ran this gift shop across from Caffeyville. Caffeyville and Kay's were demolished for construction of the four-lane highway in 1957.

CARTER & LAWSON'S - UNDERPASS CAFE AND SERVICE STATION
U. S. HWY. 66, PHILLIPSBURG, MO.

In 1941, O. E. Carter and Ed Lawson erected a prefabricated gas station just west of the Frisco Railroad overpass known as "the Subway." Many truckers had to let the air out of their tires or detour around the 13-foot-5-inch bridge. In 1950, Carter and Lawson added a café building and moved their operations here from Lebanon. The café building still stands.

The Bramhall family built the Midway Camp in 1929. John and Blanche Shank took over in 1931. The family says Bonnie Parker and Clyde Barrow stayed there for a night and complemented Blanche's cooking. This view shows the Midway after Ed and Rita Hamilton took over and expanded it into the Midway Motel in 1950.

S. W. (Sim) Harris owned all four corners at Route 66 and Route J. Central Bank now occupies the site of the Harris Modern Cabin Camp, later Conway Courts. His Standard station that became the Harris Café was where the post office is now. He owned a Shell station and a home on the other corners.

Barney Harris built a café in 1931 next to his dad's Standard station. Barney's wife Marie made the café "the Home of the Little Round Pie." This view was taken after the original building was moved to the right and expanded to include the rebuilt station. The complex was moved to the new four-lane highway in 1953 and later burned down.

Cassie Warren and his brother John opened the Top O' Th' Ozarks Café in 1940. John ran it until he entered the service. The café was leased to Mr. and Mrs. Leslie Weldon and then to Pat Ward. Orin Percy operated the station. This building burned in 1950, and Raymond Eaton established a new café between Conway and Phillipsburg.

Five

WEBSTER COUNTY

The Abbylee Court was one of the prettiest locations on Route 66 in Missouri. It opened in 1940 and consisted of eight cabins and a café, advertised as "Among the trees." The café burned in 1950, but the white clapboard cabins still stand east of the intersection with County Routes CC and M. The cabins are rented by the month.

CHICKEN & COUNTRY-HAM DINNERS
"TEXACO PRODUCTS"
35 MI. E. OF SPRINGFIELD, MO,
19 MI. W. OF LEBANON, MO.

JIMMIE O'BRIEN'S MODERN CAMP   HI-WAY 66   P.O. NIANGUA, MO.   Schuster Studio Hermann, Mo.

E 699

Jimmie O'Brien's Modern Camp was located 19 miles west of Lebanon, near Niangua. The small community was named for the Niangua River. The name is from the Native American *ne anoga*, which roughly translates to "water that runs over a man." The river flows north to form a branch of the Lake of the Ozarks.

The Garbage Can Café was seven miles east of Marshfield and seven miles west of Conway. Kermit and Letha Lowery opened the café in 1952, and a friend jokingly suggested people would remember the place if it were called the Garbage Can. The café was famous for its individual small homemade pies.

Oak Vale Park was originally known as Carpenter's, operated by Fred and Margaret Carpenter. The name was changed in 1939, and the camp operated until 1952. Oak Vale Park included cabins, a trailer park, and facilities for cooking and picnicking behind the café and gas station. Owner Alf Smith restored the house and café.

This location, adjacent to the Marshfield Golf Course and the first Marshfield Airport (1930), was originally the Main Course Filling Station and Café, later Trask's Place. Herman and Cleta Pearce opened the Skyline Café here in 1947. The site, now the Marshfield Country Club building, is the highest point on Route 66 for 900 miles.

Route 66 headed into Marshfield is known as Hubble Drive in honor of local son and astronomer Edwin Hubble. Hubble proved that the universe is expanding, the big bang theory. The Hubble space telescope was named in his honor and a one-quarter-scale copy stands in front of the courthouse. City Route 66 followed Pine Street to the square and turned west onto Washington Street.

The Marshfield Auto Court, later the Marshfield Motor Court, was originally a gas station opened by H. P. Highfill in 1930. By 1947, the station and four cabins with garages were owned by Edward Petersdorf and his son. A bank and offices now occupy the site, just east of the junction with Missouri Route 38 (West Jackson Street).

Operated by F. C. Tucker and son, the 66 Motor Court was a busy place when these photographs were taken in 1953, but its days were numbered. It closed shortly after the new four-lane Route 66 opened in 1955. The site is now a vacant field on today's Route OO west of Missouri Route 38, across from Singer Auto Parts.

The Red Top store and café opened about 1928 west of the turn-off to Northview. Eleven cabins were eventually constructed, each one with a red roof, private toilets, and individual cooking facilities. The community of Red Top also included Otto's Steak House across the highway, a feed store, a dance hall, and a tavern.

Burt and Irene Lurvey built their camp along the gravel Missouri Route 14 in 1926. It was later known as Oak Grove Lodge. The Lurveys opened a second camp in Springfield in 1928 and relocated there. The Oak Grove consisted of 14 units. Mr. and Mrs. Virgil H. Sechler owned and operated the lodge when this view was made.

The hotel on the sprawling Sam Holman ranch was popular with wealthy hunters and known for fine food long before Route 66 opened. It burned in 1961. Springfield insurance magnate John "Pat" Jones, father of Dallas Cowboys owner Jerry Jones, opened Exotic Animal Paradise here in 1971. The park offering drive-up close encounters with the animals closed in 2006 but reopened as Animal Paradise Family Fun Park in 2007.

Six

GREENE COUNTY

Strafford was featured in *Ripley's Believe it or Not* as the only town in the United States with two main streets and no back alleys. The road to the north was the main street until Route 66 was built between the backs of the businesses and the railroad. The owners simply built new entrances, giving them two front doors. (Missouri State Archives.)

Huffman's Ozark Souvenirs in Strafford was typical of the family-operated businesses once common on Route 66. Most were unassuming places, constructed from materials close at hand and offering an array of baskets, rock curios, and Ozark pottery. They were killed off by the interstate, with businesses offering mass-produced items.

Route 66 was seriously overloaded west of Strafford when this view was made in 1958. The 1926–1928 Route 66 followed present-day Missouri Route 125 south to Route YY (Division Street) and then west on Division Street to Glenstone Avenue. The post-1928 route follows today's Route OO and Missouri Route 744. (Missouri State Archives.)

4½ Miles East of Springfield, Mo., on U. S. 66

Doc's Place was originally a truck stop/café and nightclub known as the Anchor. Later known for Sunday dinners, Doc's manufactured fine homemade candies and sold novelties, gifts, souvenirs, baskets, and pottery. It advertised, "We handle the best and sell them at lower prices." The old SOMO Center, now Stiles Roofing, occupies the site.

Bungalow Court
Three miles east of Springfield, Mo.
on U. S. 66. Phone 2-4069

The Bungalow Court opened in 1946. The cabins were later linked to make up 14 family units, and it was renamed the Bungalow Motel. The pretty little pink motel closed in 1967 and became a massage parlor before being torn down in 1999. The Courts E-Plex is located on the site today.

The Victory Motor Court, with "Pure water from our own private well, 365 feet deep," opened in 1940 at 411 East Kearney Street and was operated by Mr. and Mrs. Otto Painter. New owners Mr. and Mrs. Ted Finske changed the name to Ted's in 1947. It became the Red Rooster in 1956 and later was converted to apartments.

Wallace Otto's Motel Courts offered eight "all modern fire proof steam heated cottages with locked garages" and a "popular priced café." The Bell family bought it and added eight more cabins in 1947. Lee and Jerome Carroll ran the place from 1952 into the 1990s. The office building now houses the Truck Store.

The Truck Port is on the right in this 1958 view at the east end of Springfield. It opened in the 1940s and was torn down in the 1970s for the construction of U.S. 65. A Phillips 66 station stands here today. The four-lane Route 66 bypassing Strafford and this section opened shortly after this photograph was taken. (Missouri State Archives.)

Burt and Irene Lurvey moved here from their camp east of Strafford in 1928 while the new Route 66, now Kearney Street, was still under construction. This view is from the 1950s, when Lurvey's Motel featured six sandstone-covered buildings with 12 units. The motel at 2939 East Kearney Street was converted to rentals in 1968 and is now abandoned.

Art Lurvey opened a nightclub one mile west of his brother's motel in 1942. Art had the building "rocked" and converted into the Rock View Court in 1953. It had 17 units with "Beautyrest foam pillows, modern furniture and quiet units in the back." The motel in the 2300 block of East Kearney Street was demolished for Lurvey's Plaza in 1966.

Floyd Pamplin's De Luxe Courts opened in 1930 on the northeast corner of East Kearney Street and Barnes Avenue. It had 36 units "with or without cooking facilities" and locked garages. It was later known as Ramsey Courts, Terrace Courts, and 66 East Tourist Courts before being torn down in the 1970s. Furniture Outlet stands here today.

The Eagle Tourist Court opened in 1928. It invited guests to "Sleep in Safety and Comfort without Extravagance" in the all-modern heated cottages. It offered "Prompt and Courteous Service for Our Guests," who shared a community bathroom behind the office. It stood at the southwest corner of East Kearney Street and Barnes Avenue.

Gene Finch played music outside for patrons of his drive-in at the Star Terminal. Pop Locke, owner of the neighboring Eagle Tourist Court, once blasted the speakers with a shotgun. If one was not satisfied with the food at Gene's, they would pay the check. The Star Terminal and Gene's were torn down in 1996 for a car wash.

REST HAVEN
MOTOR COURT

SPRINGFIELD, MO.

Hillary and Mary Brightwell bought Richard Chapman's gas station and opened the Rest Haven Court in 1947. The Brightwells ran the motel until 1979, adding 10 cottages to the original 4 in 1952 and 10 more in 1955. The gas station was moved behind the motel and is now used for storage. Ed Waddell did the exquisite stone and brick trim.

The current Rest Haven sign was erected in 1953 and is a favorite of photographers. Hillary Brightwell designed the sign, manufactured by Springfield Neon. Pete Hudson, owner of the Munger Moss in Lebanon, was impressed enough to adapt Brightwell's design for his motel sign. The Rest Haven is still in pristine condition today.

The Frederick family opened the Springfield Motor Court in 1946, and it was later owned by Charles and Lois Kubias. They offered modern tan brick cottages with steam heat, tile showers, and radios. They advertised large rooms and spacious grounds along with "Gyramatic Mattresses." It was torn down in 1966 for the K-Mart store.

Owned by Mr. and Mrs. Rex G. Wilson from 1940 to 1946, the Cortez boasted "All new, modern, heated cottages, kitchenette, single and double" and "Rooms at popular prices." It was torn down in 1970. From 1978 to 2007, the North Town Mall was located here. The Wal-Mart Super Center occupies the site today.

At Kearney Street and Glenstone Avenue, Route 66 travelers turned south onto Glenstone (now Business Loop 44) while Bypass 66 traffic continued ahead on Kearney (now Missouri Route 744). The Springfield Inn on the southwest corner was once the Rock Village Court, built in 1947. (Missouri State Archives.)

The Satellite Motel at 2305 North Glenstone Avenue opened in 1959, the dawn of the space age. It advertised, "27 units—hot water heat and air conditioning with room thermostat—carpeted—ceramic tile bath and free T.V." There was a heated swimming pool and playground. In 2000, it became the Raintree Inn.

Howard Williams opened the Maple Motor Court at 2233 North Glenstone Avenue in 1947. The motel advertised "Choicest Accommodations" and a tree-shaded lawn. It grew into the 32-unit Maple Motel. The restaurant specialized in "charcoal broiled steaks and fried chicken." The motel was demolished in 2006.

Mr. and Mrs. Henry Bugg said their South Winds Motor Court was "Where nice people stay for less." The native stone cabins were constructed in 1947. There were 35 units, newly decorated with "family accommodations and a playground." It became the Roy Rogers Motel in 1961 and was demolished in 1970 for a McDonald's.

The White City Tourist Park stood on this site at 2209 North Glenstone Avenue from 1927 to 1946. The Americana Motel, operated by Jean and Joan Lurvey, was built in 1959. It advertised family units, and "commercial men" were welcome. It became the Flagship Motel in 1981 and is still in business today.

The New Haven Courts invited tourists to "sleep safely." It opened at 2137 North Glenstone Avenue in 1938 and was operated by Mr. and Mrs. Otis C. Duggins. They billed the motel as the "Best in the Midwest" and noted the 12 rock-covered units were "All strictly modern, fireproof, steam heated hotel cottages."

The New Haven Courts got a major makeover in 1953. It expanded to 34 units. The gas station was removed, and a swimming pool was added. The motel was renamed the Ship and Anchor and was "air conditioned by refrigeration." The Ship and Anchor became the Ozark Motel in 1981, and it was torn down to build a Fazoli's in 1999.

The Skyline Motel opened as a tourist court "In the Heart of the Ozarks" in 1949. The 1954 AAA guide called the cabins very nice. Years later, it was extensively remodeled and expanded. The stone cottages were connected and covered with siding. It was torn down in 2004, and the site is now a car lot.

The Glenstone Cottage Court, still in business at 2023 North Glenstone Avenue, opened in 1947 and was originally know as the Greystone Cottage Court. When this view was taken, it had 14 units, 4 with kitchenettes. The units had automatic heat, television, and air-conditioning. The court has hardly changed at all over the years.

Highway department crews are working to widen the narrow Frisco Railroad underpass in this 1959 photograph. The original overpass was constructed in 1927. The view is to the north along Glenstone Avenue, toward the Glenstone Cottage Court. The billboard notes that the Rock Village Lodge was just 300 yards ahead. (Missouri State Archives.)

Al "Big Boy" Murphy opened Big Boy's Auto Court in 1937. The sign in the front read, "Hi there: Stop. We've been looking for you today." The motel became the Sands in 1959 and was torn down in 1972. The site at North Glenstone Avenue and Commercial Street is now the Brown Derby International Wine Center.

Uncle Charlie Haden's Motor Court opened in 1945 at 1801 North Glenstone Avenue. It became the Sixty-Six Motor Court in 1949. Benjamin H. and Ora M. Dickey invited visitors to "sleep in comfort in family accommodations." After Emil and Lois Grainge became owners and operators, it became the Heart of the Ozarks Motel.

Entrances and View of Headquarters Building
O'Reilly General Hospital
Springfield, Mo.

O'Reilly General Army Hospital was dedicated on November 8, 1941. Col. George B. Foster Jr. vowed to make the 155-acre facility "a hospital with a soul." Over 42,000 wounded soldiers and 60,000 dependents were treated before O'Reilly closed on August 28, 1952. The Assemblies of God Church opened Evangel University here in 1955.

The Lily-Tulip Corporation chose Springfield as the site for its new plant in December 1951. The plant with its giant "cup" entrance employed up to 1,200 people at one time. Sold to Owens-Illinois in 1968, it was sold to a newly formed Lily-Tulip in 1981 and became Sweetheart Cup in 1989. (Missouri State Archives.)

Carl Hamby and his partners built the Restwell Motel in 1947 at the corner of North Glenstone Avenue and Pythian Street, across from O'Reilly General Army Hospital. The Restwell touted television, telephones, steam heat, air-conditioning, and carpeting. The Restwell was in business until 1986, and a car wash occupies the site today.

John and Hazel Baldridge opened their motor court in 1939. They remodeled and changed the name to the Silver Saddle Motel in 1957. In 1997, it became the Dogwood Inn. The 1960s City Route 66 turned west on Chestnut Street to West College Avenue while the main route continued south on Glenstone Avenue, turning west on St. Louis Street.

One of the gems of Route 66 started out as eight tiny stone cabins surrounded by a rail fence built in 1938 by Lawrence and Elwyn Lippman. The greatly expanded complex became the Rail Haven Motel in 1954. Ward Chrisman bought the Rail Haven in 1961 and added the Sycamore Restaurant. Gordon Elliott tore down the closed restaurant and completely renovated the fading Rail Haven after taking over in 1994.

This 1956 view looks north on Glenstone Avenue from St. Louis Street toward the 1939 viaduct over the Frisco Railroad. Sanders Standard Service (now Scott's Route 66 Service) is on the far right. The Rail Haven Motel is on the left. The service station on the left was originally Huffman's Tydol, later Wallace D-X. (Missouri State Archives.)

The Manhattan Dinner House at the southeast corner of Glenstone Avenue and St. Louis Street opened in 1947 and closed in the 1960s. It advertised "good wholesome food, nicely served." The Manhattan specialized in steaks. Cash Advance occupies the building today.

In August 1953, a disgruntled youth released 12 deadly hooded Indian cobras from exotic animal dealer Reo Mowrer's shop in the 1400 block of St. Louis Street. The city was terrorized for two months until all the snakes were captured or killed. Police played snake charmer music on loudspeakers hoping to lure them out. Cobras are actually deaf!

Gus Belt opened the first Steak n' Shake Restaurant in Bloomington, Illinois, in 1934. The steak burgers have always been prepared right in front of diners, with the slogan "In Sight it Must be Right." This location at St. Louis Street (Route 66) and North National Avenue opened in 1963 and looks much the same today. (Steak n' Shake.)

The Kentwood Arms Hotel was built in 1926 by John T. Woodruff, a developer and first president of the U.S. Highway 66 Association. It had over 100 units and a rooftop terrace garden. Southwest Missouri State, now Missouri State University, acquired the building in 1984. It is now the Kentwood Hall dormitory.

The Abou Ben Adhem Shrine Mosque was billed as the largest auditorium west of the Mississippi when dedicated on November 3, 1923. Architects Heckenlively and Mark designed the building in Saracenic, or Moorish, style. In 1956, Elvis Presley played the Shrine. Harry Truman, Franklin Roosevelt, and Ronald Reagan also appeared there.

Pierce Petroleum Bus and Tourist Terminal
U. S. Highway 66, Springfield, Mo.

The first of the lavish Pierce-Petroleum Terminals in the Ozarks opened in Springfield on July 16, 1928. The facility included a restaurant, gas station, and even a car wash. It became the Greyhound bus station in 1936 and was demolished in 1979. The site is now the parking lot for the Discovery Center.

This 1953 view looks west along St. Louis Street from Kimbrough Avenue. The Greyhound bus depot is on the left. The Martin Chrysler-Plymouth building site is now the Discovery Center. Dee's Liquor and the Hotel Moran are on the right. The Woodruff Building is in the background on the right, across from the Colonial Hotel.

This is a view of the north side of St. Louis Street about 1965. The Motor Inn Downtown was originally the Fraternity Building, built by John T. Woodruff in 1914. It was the Hotel Ozarks from 1923 to 1945 and the Hotel Moran from 1946 to 1962. The whole block was demolished in 1973, and U.S. Bank is located here today.

The Colonial Hotel, constructed in 1907 on the southwest corner of St. Louis Street and Jefferson Avenue, was the first steel-framed multistory building in Springfield. Harry Truman, Elvis Presley, and John F. Kennedy stayed here. The creation of a pedestrian mall on Route 66 in 1973 killed the Colonial. It closed in 1978 and was torn down in 1998.

The Woodruff Building opened on February 1, 1911, the same day the Republican and Frisco Buildings were opened. It contained 276 offices, a drugstore, barbershop, and pool hall. At John T. Woodruff's office here on April 30, 1926, the number 66 was reportedly first proposed for the highway between Chicago and Los Angeles.

In 1926, M. E. Gillioz could not find a spot on the proposed highway for his new theater. So he bought property one block north, leased a 20-foot-wide frontage on St. Louis Street, and linked it to the theater 130 feet away. Elvis Presley watched a movie here before his 1956 concert. The 1,100-seat Gillioz closed in 1980. The Springfield Landmarks Preservation Trust restored the theater and reopened it in 2006. (Tom Bradley.)

This 1940s view of the square shows Heer's Department Store (1915–1995) and the Lander's Building. The "pie" in the middle was in place from 1909 until 1947. A historical marker is located where James "Wild Bill" Hickock killed Dave Tutt in a duel over a gambling debt on July 21, 1865.

This view looks north in 1949, after the "pie" was removed. St. Louis Street (Route 66) entered from the right and continued straight through, exiting on the left as College Street. This configuration was in place until 1973, when the square became a pedestrian mall. That layout changed in 1999, and the route now travels around Park Central to College Street. (Missouri State Archives.)

The Rockwood Court and Cafe opened in 1929. It advertised, "All units new—one of the finest and most beautiful courts in the city on Highway 66." It was "Strictly modern, tubs and shower, tile baths." The café became Ginny Lee's Restaurant in 1969, but was operating under the Rockwood Court Café name again in 2009.

ROCK FOUNTAIN COURT
On Hwy. 66, 166, 60 and 13. "City Route"
Springfield, Missouri
One of Springfield's Finest

The Rock Fountain Court at 2400 West College Street stands as a fine example of the work done by rock man Ed Waddell. Waddell also worked on the Rock Village, Rock Fountain, and Trail's End motels. In 1961, new owner Sherman Nutt named it Melinda Court after his daughter.

Frank Campbell started a trucking company in Springfield during the 1920s. His firm merged with 66 Rapid Express in 1933 to become Campbell's 66 Express. The trucks featuring the galloping camel Snortin' Norton and the motto "Humpin' to Please" were a familiar sight for over 55 years. Two Campbell 66 Express 18-wheelers can be seen today at Rich Henry's Rabbit Ranch in Staunton, Illinois.

Sheldon "Red" Chaney ran out of room for the "ER" on the sign, so his café became Red's Giant "Hamburg." Red's was home to what may have been the first drive-up restaurant window in the United States. It was featured twice in *Rolling Stone* and immortalized in song by the Morells. Red and his wife Julia closed down on December 14, 1984, and Red's was demolished in 1999. (Cathy Hickman and Tom Carter, Ozarks Public Television.)

Roy and Marie Farley operated the Bypass Terminal Café at the junction of City 66 (Chestnut Street) and Bypass 66. They sold Barnsdall gas and had rooms for rent upstairs. The sign advertises Royal Crown Cola, "Best by Taste Test." It was torn down in the 1970s, and a Kum n' Go convenience store occupies the site today.

A "Homelike Atmosphere You Will Always Remember" was promised at the Wishing Well Motel. The motel opened in 1947 with 17 units, on beautifully landscaped grounds. The wishing well at the center is long gone, but the motel is still in business today at 3550 Chestnut Expressway.

The Sunset Court was just west of the junction of City 66 and Bypass 66. Some of the units were equipped for cooking. The rates were $2 for one person and $3 for two when this card was published in the 1940s. The court was torn down in 1980, and a Sonic drive-in restaurant is located here now.

The Thunderbird Motel was originally the Red Bird Camp and then the Redbird Motel, "The motel with the tree growing through the roof." Ruth and Lyle Breyer changed the name to the Thunderbird in 1961. The motel closed in 1980 and Continental Carbonic occupies the site. Note the nice Thunderbird automobile out front.

In 1944, Leonard and Wilma Greer turned their home two and a half miles west of Springfield into the Lone Star Tourist Court, with modern cabins, a café, and a Standard station with a fine selection of penny candy. The Best Budget Inn was built on the site at 4421 Chestnut Expressway in 1990.

Heading straight west on Kearney Street at Glenstone Avenue put travelers on Bypass 66. The street was named for Frisco Railroad official Michael Kearney. Immediately west of Glenstone, the Rancho Motel has been in business since 1955. The site was originally the Allied Service Travel Court.

The Trail's End Motor Court (later just motel) at 1534 East Kearney Street opened in 1949 and had a beautiful neon sign featuring a Native American. J. H. Miller owned the classic Ozark stone motel when this view was made. The motel closed in 1989, and the Native American on the sign is gone. Now the Rancho Court Apartments, the units are rented by the month.

Star Lite Court & Cafe
**1231 W. KEARNEY ST., HIWAYS 66-166 & 13 BY-PASS,
SPRINGFIELD, MISSOURI**

The Star Lite Court opened in 1953 and was owned by Ed and Gladys Spence. Their motto was "Service and courtesy." They billed the motel as "New, Ultra Modern" with "Steam Heat, Beauty Rest Sleep, Tile Showers," and reasonable rates. The court was torn down in 1980, and the China Castle Restaurant is located here today.

This 1951 view shows Bypass 66 (Kearney Street) at Melville Road. The Stuffed Pig Café and Motel was here from 1940 until 1968. Owner Johnny Weatherwax reportedly got the stuffed pig recipe while serving in France during World War I. He was killed in a robbery at his motel. The bypass route continues west on Kearney (Missouri Route 744) to the West Bypass (U.S. 160) and turns south to meet the main route. (Missouri State Archives.)

Ben Brewer built six cabins of native stone in 1935. Graystone Heights grew to "Eight modern cabins and café, air cooled, Conoco Service" by the time Shorty West was running it a few years later. Mr. and Mrs. Art Brummer later owned the business. The buildings at 9323 Missouri Route 266 are now used by R&S Floral.

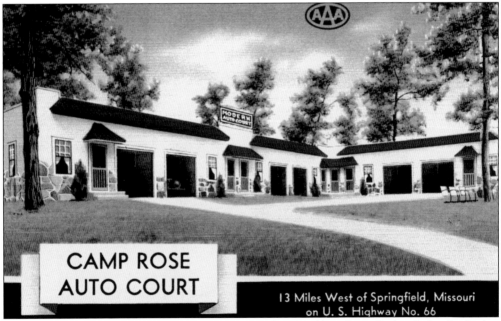

Allan Rose chose "One of the coolest spots in the Ozarks," above Pickerel Creek, for his automobile court. The motel was "Away from all noise and railroad" and offered "Good water, playgrounds for children, popular priced coffee shop." The site was Sam Holman's H Dude Ranch during the 1960s and is now a private home.

Seven

LAWRENCE COUNTY

Route 66 in Lawrence County is known as the "ghost section" for its numerous roadside ruins. This view looks west on Route 66 from the eastern outskirts of Halltown in 1954. Halltown once called itself the "Antiques Capital of the World" and boasted over 20 businesses during the Route 66 era. (Missouri State Archives.)

A few businesses hang on in Halltown, notably the Whitehall Mercantile on the right. The building with the false front dates back to 1900. The former Las Vegas Hotel and Café is on the left. Charlie Dammer built the hotel in 1930 after he hit it big in Las Vegas. West of Halltown, the old road continues straight ahead at Missouri Route 96.

Fred Mason opened his station at Paris Springs in 1930 and named it Gay Parita after his wife. *Parita* means "equal," and Fred and Gay were equal partners. Gay died in 1953, and Fred carried on until the station burned down in 1955. Fred never rebuilt and retired to the couple's beautiful fieldstone dream home on the property. He died in 1960. (Gary Turner.)

Gary Turner constructed a replica Sinclair station at Gay Parita in 2007. The Masons' original cobblestone garage still stands. Turner is a great ambassador for Route 66, and Gay Parita is a stop no traveler should miss.

When Sidney Casey learned of plans for the new highway in 1925, he paid $400 for the "town" of Spencer, a vacant store and two acres of land. The complex grew to include a café, barbershop, service station, and garage. It all closed when the highway was rerouted in 1961. Sidney Casey's son Carl is shown here at the station in 1946. The buildings still stand and are being restored. (Route 66 Association of Missouri.)

CAMP LOOKOUT

Camp Lookout was 24 miles west of Springfield and 33 miles east of Carthage, the "Most Modern on U.S. 66." It was also billed as "Your Home Away From Home" and as "spotlessly clean." The camp included nine cottages, a café, and a gas station. Only the station and café foundations remain today.

This 1952 crash near Camp Lookout was not the worst disaster on this part of Route 66. In the 1950s, towns in this area threatened to sue if they lost the U.S. 66 designation to the new Interstate 44. So the government built Interstate 44 to the south, completely bypassing the area and killing businesses. The Route 66 signs came down anyway in 1972. (Missouri State Archives.)

Ed and Mary Lewis, former owners of the Grandview, had just bought the Traveler's Lodge when they mailed this card in 1952. They offered souvenirs and "novelties from the Ozarks, groceries and all travel needs." Mary said they were "quite the farmers" with four cows and four calves on their 20 acres.

This photograph was taken in March 1955, just before the highway department realigned Route 66 through Phelps and demolished the buildings on the south side, including the Texaco station and café run by Mr. and Mrs. Harry Parkhurst. Their house was later moved to Route 66 in Albatross. (Reva Hunt West, Lynda West Hahn collection.)

Mr. and Mrs. Roy Rogers built these cabins and a station at Rescue in the 1920s. (They were not related to the famous cowboy.) It was later known as Reed's Cabin Court and is now a private residence. In 1961, the Rogers family bought the Southwinds Motor Court in Springfield and renamed it the Roy Rogers Motel. The community earned the name Rescue when the locals took in a family headed west after their wagon broke down.

Shady Side Camp was built by L. F. Arthur about 1927 amid a beautiful stand of oak trees. In 1935, the four stone cottages rented for $1 to $1.50 per night. The camp advertised "private cooking facilities, dishes not provided, and access to community toilets and showers." It is now a private residence, and some cabins still stand.

Eight

JASPER COUNTY

Carl Stansbury built Log City in 1926 with trees cut from the property. By the time of this 1938 view, it had 14 modern cottages. It advertised, "Dining room and coffee shop air-conditioned by washed air." It grew to 16 units, 3 of which still stand. The station building became a body shop. There was a complex called Stone City just to the west.

Forest Park Camp, with 10 stone cabins, was opened by Whitson and Hammond in 1928. The owners of Forest Park Camp and Log City were always trying to outdo their competitors across the highway, constantly adding amenities and cutting prices. Joplin Truss now occupies the Forest Park Camp location, and just one small rock building remains.

The "ghost section" of Route 66 passes through Avilla, where this shot of highway department crews spreading mulch was taken in 1954. Avilla was hit particularly hard by the arrival of the interstate, and many of the businesses are now roadside ruins. (Missouri State Archives.)

White's Court

EAST JUNCTION U. S. HIGHWAYS 66 AND 71 CARTHAGE, MO.

White's Court started out as a café and gas station about 1927. The eight cabins were added later. The Scotts bought the court in 1957, enclosed the cottages and garages, and ran it until 1987. They advertised "Modern cottages. Café in connection. We service your car." It is now the Red Rock Apartments.

The Buster Brown Inn was owned by E. J. Brown. The building still stands, across from the Red Rock Apartments on the east side of Lake Kellogg. In the 1950s, Route 66 was realigned to follow what is now Missouri Route 96. The Sportsmen's Protective League constructed Lake Kellogg between the old Route 66 and the new highway.

The Lake Shore Motel advertised excellent fishing on Lake Kellogg. Owner J. K. Bunk's motto was "Wonderful Rest in Cleanliness." Mr. and Mrs. Frank Tucker were running the motel when this view was taken in 1964. The Lake Shore is now the Best Budget Inn.

AAA recommended the Kel-Lake Motel, also across from Lake Kellogg. Ernest J. Jackson ran the motel from 1955 until 1965. Jackson was known for helping the less-fortunate travelers. The construction of Interstate 44 prompted Jackson to sell, but the Kel-Lake hung on. The motel is still in business today.

During the 1930s and 1940s, Route 66 followed what is now Route V to today's Missouri Route 571, entering the city over three viaducts spanning the Spring River and the railroad. The $205,000 bridges were dedicated in June 1930. The route later shifted to follow today's Missouri Route 96/Central Avenue, Garrison Avenue, and Oak Street.

The C and W Café was operated by Mr. and Mrs. Bus White and Mr. and Mrs. Ray Carter. It opened in 1935 on the north side of the square and later moved to the east side. They advertised as "A Friendly Place to Eat. Good Food—Moderately Priced. Completely Air Conditioned" and used "Cornfed U.S. Steer Beef Exclusively."

Carthage was established in 1842 and named for the great ancient city of North Africa. The rebel Missouri State Guard won a victory in an early Civil War battle north of town on July 5, 1861. The rebels burned the town in 1864. Carthage was also home to the notorious Belle Starr, the "Bandit Queen." The courthouse dates from 1895.

Red Danner opened his café at Central and Garrison Avenues on August 19, 1941. Whatever kind of meat customers left on their plate would be mashed together and served again as the house special meatloaf. A rare 1936 Chicago Coin's Band-Box from Red's, with miniature band figures playing *Route 66*, is now displayed at C.D.'s Pancake Hut, 301 Garrison.

Arthur Boots built one of the most famous landmarks on Route 66 at the intersection with U.S. 71 in 1939. Clark Gable once stayed in room number six. The Neelys bought it in 1942 and added the rear units. Ruben and Rachel Asplin took over in 1948, and Rachel ran the Boots until she died in 1991. The motel has been converted to apartments.

Arthur Boots designed another deco moderne building for his drive-in restaurant across the street. The Boots Drive-In and Gift Shop opened in 1946 "At the Crossroads of America." It offered breakfast at any hour and sold souvenirs and novelties. The Boots closed in 1970 and is now the Great Plains Credit Union.

TAYLOR TOURIST PARK
Carthage, Mo.

SEASON OF 1931-'32.

Type of modern cottages at TAYLOR PARK, one quarter mile west of Carthage, Mo., on both Highways 66 and 71.

Dr. C. B. Taylor opened his tourist park in 1927. His son-in-law, H. C. Scoville, took over the Taylor Tourist Park shortly before the doctor died in 1931. For many years, it was known as the Park Motor Court and Café, named after the park across the street. The Powers Museum opened on this site in 1988.

F. Naramore and W. D. Bradfield's 66 Drive-In opened on September 22, 1949, showing *Two Guys from Texas*. It closed in 1985 and became a salvage yard. Mark Goodman reopened the drive-in on April 3, 1997. It is the only survivor of six drive-ins that once bore the 66 name.

Carterville once boasted a population of 12,000 but was devastated when the mines closed after World War I. This view of Main Street looks west. The Weeks Hardware Building, now Morton Booth Company, is at left center. Note the double trolley tracks. Route 66 followed Pine Street, Main Street, and Carter Street to Broadway.

Webb City was the heart of the tristate mining district. There were 50 mines operating during World War I, and the population peaked at 28,000. The Sucker Flats mining area at center is now King Jack Park. (*Jack* is slang for zinc ore.) The park is home to the *Praying Hands*, created by Jack Dawson. The hands are 32 feet tall and weigh 110 tons. (Missouri State Archives.)

117

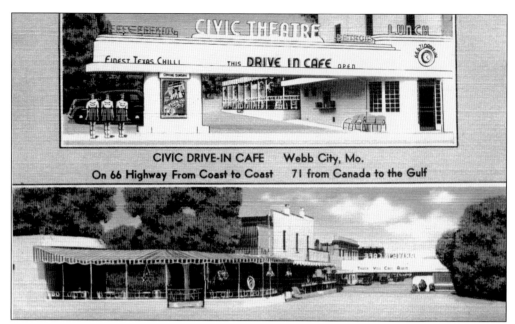

CIVIC DRIVE-IN CAFE   Webb City, Mo.
On 66 Highway From Coast to Coast   71 from Canada to the Gulf

Larry P. Larsen designed over 100 theaters, including the Fox Theatre in Joplin. He also designed the Civic Drive-In Café in Webb City, "Tri-State's only Dry Night Club and Restaurant." The open-air restaurant was later enclosed, and it became an office building. Route 66 followed Broadway, with a brief jog at Webb Street west of Main Street.

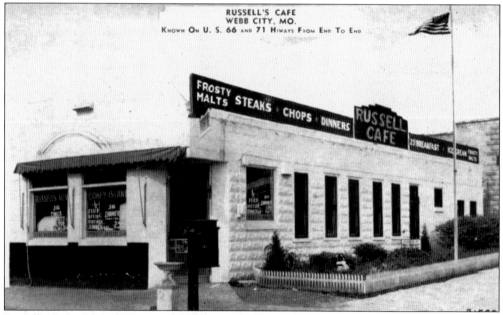

Russell's Café claimed to serve 100,000 people per year in the 1940s. It was demolished about 1980. Route 66 through Joplin originally followed Madison Street, Zora Street, Florida Avenue, Utica Street, and Euclid Avenue. It merged onto St. Louis Street and then turned onto Broadway and Main Street before heading west on Seventh Street. In 1930, the route shifted to follow Broadway, Powell Drive, and MacArthur Drive to Main Street.

410 SO. MADISON AVE., WEBB CITY, MO.

The Ozark Motel was owned by Mr. and Mrs. Harold Fenix when this view was made. Mr. and Mrs. Herman Davis later operated the motel, which was in operation from 1951 to 1968. A McDonald's stands here today at 410 South Madison Street. At Broadway, Bypass 66 turned south on Madison, which turns into Range Line Road.

Joplin began as two lawless and feuding mining camps, Joplin City and Murphysburg, combined in 1873. Looking south on Main Street, the Hotel Connor at right opened in 1908. Two workers died, and one was trapped for 82 hours when the building collapsed during demolition on November 11, 1978. The Joplin Library stands here today. The building at far left was once the House of Lords, an infamous saloon, gambling house, and brothel.

The Keystone Motel at Fourth and Main Street opened in 1892. It was built by E. Z. Wallower, a Pennsylvania newspaper publisher, and named in honor of his home state. Wallower and Connor Hotel owner Thomas Connor were intense rivals. The Keystone was torn down in 1968.

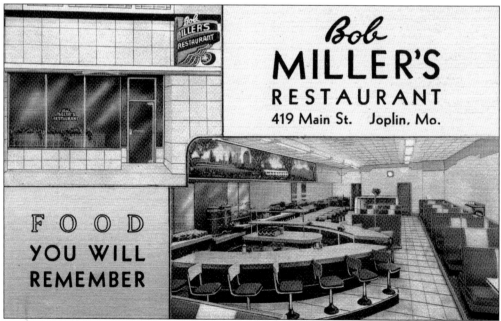

Bob Miller's first café was at 609 Main Street. He opened this restaurant at 419 Main Street on the original site of the Heidelberg Inn after World War II. Ultramodern pigmented structural glass was used on the exterior facade, the counters, and the floors. The restaurant closed in the 1990s, and the site is now an office building.

"Joplin's Newest and Finest Tourist Motel"

If travelers chose the bypass route via Range Line Road, they passed by the Fenix Ultra Modern Motel, also built by the family that constructed the Ozark Motel. They boasted of the 15-acre shady lawn as "the Crossroads of America." A hair salon last occupied the building at 2710 North Range Line Road.

On Highways 66 & 71, East City Limits, Joplin, Mo.

"The Place to Sleep," the Twin Oaks Court at Range Line Road and Fourth Street also offered "Just Good Food." In 1954, AAA said the Twin Oaks was "a very good court on spacious shaded grounds." The site is now a Blimpie sub shop.

The path of Route 66 through Joplin shifted many times, often due to collapsing mine shafts. The final route followed Range Line Road south, turning west on Seventh Street (now Missouri Route 66). In this 1952 view west on Seventh Street, the Elms Motel property is at right. The Forest Park Baptist Church lot is on the left. (Missouri State Archives.)

The Elms Motel advertised as "Joplin's Finest," with 25 "beautifully furnished fireproof cottages on spacious grounds." It also boasted of "Wall to wall carpeting, tile showers, free radios, vented wall heaters and individual telephones." The Elms closed in 1964, and a Toys "R" Us store occupies this site today.

A 1953 view of Seventh Street (Route 66) between Michigan and School Streets shows the Meeker Building at left. Meeker was one of the largest manufacturers of leather products such as billfolds and purses. The reinforced concrete and brick building opened in 1927. The factory closed in 1987 and was demolished in 1995. (Missouri State Archives.)

Mr. and Mrs. A. C. Jergens were owners of the East Seventh Street Motel when this view was made about 1957. The motel at 1902 East Seventh originally consisted of 17 units. It had grown to 22 units, with steam heat and free television, by 1957. The sign said kitchenettes and baby beds were available. Bob Owens Auto Center is located here today.

The Plaza Motel was owned by F. Van Pelt and his son when this card was issued. It advertised "Twenty-one luxuriously furnished units, carpeting, tubs or showers, tile baths, refrigerated air-panel ray heat, free TV, free coffee bar and cubed ice." The Plaza is still in business today at 2612 East Seventh Street.

Roy Hemphill opened Roy's on South Main Street in the 1930s. He moved to West Seventh Street about 1939. Charles Keller purchased the business in 1948 and changed the name to Keller's in the early 1950s. "Meet your friends here" was its slogan. Keller's specialized in fried chicken, barbecue ribs, and thick malts.

Harry M. Bennett's Koronado Hotel Kourts were the "Finest and Most Up-to-Date Tourist Kourts in the Entire Southwest on U.S. 66 Highway." The travelers who sent this card noted that all 60 units were filled that night. They also commented on a huge slag heap across the street. The Wal-Mart Super Center occupies this site today.

The Little King's Hotel Court had 60 rooms and 75 double beds. One could pick up information here about the famous "Spook Light." The strange bouncing light has been appearing in the tristate area since the Quapaw Indian days. No one has been able to find an explanation. The Little King's site is now occupied by a cellular telephone company.

CASTLE MOTEL
HIWAY U. S. 66 W. — JOPLIN, MO.

The Castle Motel, originally Castle Kourt, was located at 2403 West Seventh Street, where Fashion Bug is today. It originally had 24 cabins, later 35 units. The traveler who sent this card wrote, "This is the most pleasant tourist court I have ever stopped at. For $2 with a garage for the car it is certainly worth the money."

Mickey Mantle grew up in nearby Commerce, Oklahoma, and played shortstop for the Joplin Miners in 1950. Mantle is posed in the Dugout Lounge at his Holiday Inn on South Range Line Road. Motels with space-age designs like the Riviera, Thunderbird, and Rocket sprang up there when Interstate 44 opened in 1957. They advertised locations on the "66 Bypass," although Route 66 never officially went south of Seventh Street.

The name of this traveler posed at the Missouri-Kansas state line is lost. The sign indicates the mileage to Galena, Kansas; Miami, Oklahoma; and Tulsa, Oklahoma. There are 13.2 miles of Route 66 in Kansas, all of which was bypassed when the Will Rogers Turnpike opened on June 28, 1957. (Larry Davidson and Anne Rains.)

This was the scene for Route 66 travelers ending their journey across Missouri. The business on the Kansas side was selling Coca-Cola. But since Kansas was a dry state, there were plenty of businesses on the Missouri side offering something a little stronger. The State Line Bar and Grill, just inside Missouri, is a notable survivor. (Laurel Kane.)

DISCOVER THOUSANDS OF LOCAL HISTORY BOOKS FEATURING MILLIONS OF VINTAGE IMAGES

Arcadia Publishing, the leading local history publisher in the United States, is committed to making history accessible and meaningful through publishing books that celebrate and preserve the heritage of America's people and places.

Find more books like this at
www.arcadiapublishing.com

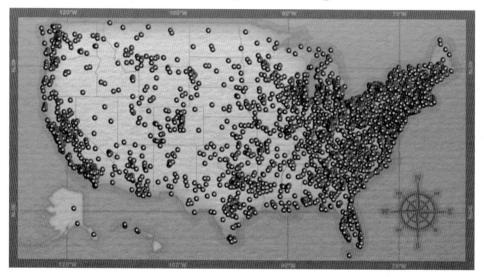

Search for your hometown history, your old stomping grounds, and even your favorite sports team.

Consistent with our mission to preserve history on a local level, this book was printed in South Carolina on American-made paper and manufactured entirely in the United States. Products carrying the accredited Forest Stewardship Council (FSC) label are printed on 100 percent FSC-certified paper.

MADE IN THE USA